American Poverty

By Laurel A. Rockefeller

I0455294

Laurel A. Rockefeller

TABLE OF CONTENTS

INTRODUCTION

In 2014 when this book was first written, the world was a different place. We were six years into the largely successful presidency of Barack Obama, a man of such integrity that not a single scandal tainted his eight years in office. Obama was deeply respected and, more importantly, trusted by both allies and enemies alike. When Obama promised to help the Ukraine defend itself against Russian aggressions, the people there knew his word was good as gold and that help would be coming—without consideration for what was personally beneficial to Obama.

It was a different era, the last presidency when the United States of America was regarded as a trusted superpower. Where the United States lead, other countries followed.

But it was not perfect. Poor domestic policy decisions made by both Congress and the US presidency over the last forty years has created unprecedented income inequities that challenge longstanding myths about the poor and the nature of poverty. Times have changed. Our challenges have changed, but American attitudes towards the poor have not changed—at least not for the better. Programs like Society Security and Medicare are treated as "entitlements," as charity if you will, rather than the pre-paid benefits that they actually are. Terms like "socialism" and "democratic socialism" remain feared instead of embraced. Unions remain weak. The buying power of a minimum-wage paying job worked forty hours per week is at an all-time low.

American Poverty

In this book, I highlight American Poverty culture. In part one, I explore five different facets as written in a series of essays originally written for and published by Yahoo Voices between 2012 and 2014. In part two, I look at each of these five topics systematically to see what the best available economic, social science, and political science data has to offer. Finally, I examine how conditions in Germany, Canada, France, and the United Kingdom differ from those in the United States.

Though many things have changed since I initially wrote my analysis in 2014, (case in point, David Cameron is no longer the Prime Minister of the United Kingdom), in most details the conditions in Germany, Canada, France, and the UK remain constant and will continue to for as long as each of these countries remain dedicated to human rights.

It is my sincerest hope that the United States will learn from the examples of its best allies so that the poorest and most disadvantaged Americans may yet live with dignity, access to healthcare without risking financial hardship, and with certain and ready access to all the essentials of life, including safe and clean drinking water. We all deserve nothing less.

PART ONE: ESSAYS

A Lack of Empathy: originally published on 2nd May, 2012 on Yahoo Voices.

Less Than Human: originally published on 16th September, 2013 on Yahoo Voices.

Shaming Poverty: originally published on 3rd November, 2013 on Yahoo Voices.

Public Housing: originally published 12th May, 2014 on Yahoo Voices.

Poverty and the Problem of Blurred Lines

A Lack of Empathy: Increased Self-Reliance at the Expense of Social-consciousness

It's a mental health epidemic. It's a change in how people conduct themselves socially. It's been worsening every year since the 1980s. It has created enormous misery in our society. It is…our increasing lack of empathy for other people, our inability to "walk in another's shoes."

Declining empathy is one of those social subjects we all seem to be aware of on some level-yet rarely understand enough about to make the needed changes. At Psychology and Society's website[1] we see a psychologist's concept of empathy, "a vicarious emotional experience in which you feel and understand what another person feels … there are two elements of empathy: perspective taking (understanding what another person feels), and vicarious emotion (feeling what another person feels)."

This means that we not only experience another's feelings (psychologists consider that "sympathy") but truly UNDERSTAND where the other person is coming from. It is both a cognitive and emotional response to another person.

In Wicca, psychic empaths experience another's feelings and experiences very tangibly, often experiencing other people's pains and sorrows more

---

[1] http://www.psychologyandsociety.com/empathydefinition.html

intensely than those people experience them on a conscious level, picking up on their unconscious and subconscious experiences in addition to the conscious ones each individual readily conveys.

This "feel within" experience is critical to our ability to help others. Entrepreneur Mark S. Birch discusses Empathy in American history in his article, "Empathy and the American Dilemma[2]" describing the evolution of the American middle class and why the "Greatest Generation" experienced far more empathy for others than we do today.

His article is an enlightening journey through history, helping us to understand how we moved from a culture of shared social responsibility to "generation me" where "greed is good." The "Greatest Generation" was more empathic than we are today because of the common experiences everyone shared in the Great Depression and WWII which served as great social equalizers.

Mark Birch describes that during depression, "People were standing in soup kitchen lines as equals. People worked alongside each other building the next generation of national infrastructure." He goes on to describe how during the 1980s, "The political dynamic changed as well to reflect this growing self-reliance. This meant initiatives to lower taxes, shrink government, reduce regulation, and dismantle welfare policies."

By the 1980s, our sense of caring and helping others that was forged so intensely by the shared experiences of the 1930s and 1940s had severely eroded.

---

[2] http://birch.co/post/11653486193/empathy-and-the-american-dilemma

American Poverty

Now we live in "Generation Me" where greed is so pervasive and regulation so weak that, as it was during the 1920s[3] those who could manipulate financial systems and profit from them exploited them to the point where both housing and financial industries collapsed. After years of focusing on just ourselves, we are ill-equipped psychologically to help others, to put our profits, our wants, our interests aside and look at the world through someone else's eyes.

We see this in our daily lives in the increase of rudeness, the increase of casual violence, and even just our inability to maintain social relationships for long periods of time. We marry thinking we can make the other person serve our selfish interests-and when they don't, we discard the relationship, divorce, and look for someone else.

Just think how much better your life could be if you and everyone around you learned what our parents, grandparents, and great grand-parents from the Greatest Generation learned: we are all connected, every life is valuable, every life (human, plant, and animal) is precious, every viewpoint is valid. When we transcend our petty momentary desires, we find ourselves and our world enriched. Empathy evolved among humans because it fosters life. We need each other and we need communities. Let us all endeavour think before we speak, look at life through the view-points of others, and care about those around us.

---

[3] PBS: *The American Experience*: "The Crash of 1929"
http://www.pbs.org/wgbh/americanexperience/features/transcript/crash-transcript/

Less than Human: Complacency, Poverty, and Human Rights

A Look at Conditions Face by and Attitudes Regarding the Poor and Unemployed

Sunday 1st of September, 2013 1st was a beautiful day. A friend came over and together we went to an area golf driving range, my first opportunity to leave my home for a reason other than grocery shopping or job interviews in over six months. After a full year of not practicing, my hits were off, but I enjoyed the practice, never thinking anything was wrong with using the natural grass section to learn how to hit a golf ball off an actual tee.

Monday, 2nd of September, the first bites came. I changed my bedding and started the arduous process of trying to hand wash my sheets; still clueless fleas hitched a ride in my things and on me while golfing. Until, that is, around one a.m. on Wednesday morning when twelve bites woke me. Using a flashlight I found the culprits: fleas! At dawn, I stripped the bed and started washing, the other set of sheets barely dry. At as soon the management office for my public housing community opened, I phoned the manager and asked for help with the bugs, spending all of the day washing as best I could from a bucket and leaving 90% of my blankets unwashed for the lack of access to washing machines.

American Poverty

Thursday 5th of September, the exterminator came. When I spoke to him, he chided me for vacuuming my bed[4], one of the well-established techniques[5] advocated in a multi-pronged approach to eliminate fleas. Instead, he insisted it had to be bed bugs, despite my descriptions of what I found each day and despite my solid research (which included his company's own website).

When he found my bed clean of bed bugs, he seemed almost mad at me, especially as I asserted myself and asked him politely to please spray for fleas. Even showing him my dozens of bites did no good. It never entered this man's mind that I could be intelligent, educated, and pro-active about my life — just because of where I live right now. Just because I am poor and still unemployed.

Poverty and unemployment does not signal a lack of intelligence. It does not mean a person dropped out of school. It does not make a person a drug addict, drug dealer, or even an unwed parent creating child after child to collect government benefits. Poverty doesn't make a person mentally or even physically deficient in any way.

Poverty only means a person lacks money sufficient to provide food, healthcare, proper housing, and so forth. Unemployment simply means you are looking for work and have not found it yet. No more!

---

[4] http://www2.ca.uky.edu/entomology/entfacts/ef602.asp

[5] http://citybugs.tamu.edu/factsheets/biting-stinging/others/ent-3001/

Are there people who are unemployed or are poor because of some sort of "deficit" such as just described? Yes, of course. But any connection between the aforementioned and poverty/unemployment remains limited. That is some poor people deal drugs. Some poor people have different fathers/mothers for each of their children. Some poor people have some sort of mental or physical challenge.

The problem socially is the bad habit of generalizing to the overwhelming majority of the poor, unemployed, and working poor who do none of those things.

These are the people who work for minimum wage. These are the moderately disabled like me who have physical limits due to accident, injury, and/or illness — but do not meet the Federal definitions[6] for "permanently disabled." These are the huge numbers of people laid off by the Great Recession from industries and in geography still waiting for the recovery[7] to start.

We number in the millions[8].

So why are we less than human?

Less than human because we need nutritional assistance[9]. This means struggling to feed our

---

[6] http://www.ssab.gov/documents/socialsecuritydefinitionofdisability.pdf

[7] http://www.huffingtonpost.com/2013/06/07/long-term-unemployed-jobs-report_n_3402015.html?1370614437

[8] http://data.bls.gov/timeseries/LNS14000000

[9] http://thesocietypages.org/socimages/2012/09/03/food-stamps-public-policy-and-the-working-poor/

families[10] on the meagre allowances from food stamp programs constantly assaulted by politicians who feel "entitlements" such as food are not deserved by those receiving them. This means our children failing in school because school-based nutritional help reaches too few children on too few days of the year. This means obesity[11] created by a lack of whole, fresh food availability.

Less than human because we cannot afford pristine houses with big yards. Instead, large numbers of us live in sub-standard apartments, public housing, and subsidized housing. These homes tend to be cold in the winter and hot in the summer. They amplify and transmit noise from neighbours. They distribute toxic air from neighbours, traffic, and beyond. Inadequate, infrequent vermin prevention and treatment leads to disease and misery such as mine.

Less than human because employers assume internal defects[12], not the recession, create long term unemployment, compounding the problem and ignoring the talents and professional backgrounds of the long term unemployed. Recent job gains in low-paying sectors mean most of those previously laid off and now in new jobs now work too few hours for too little pay[13] to afford the most basic of human dignities.

---

[10] http://www.feedingamerica.org/

[11] http://diabetes.diabetesjournals.org/content/60/11/2667.full

[12] http://www.huffingtonpost.com/2013/06/07/long-term-unemployed-jobs-report_n_3402015.html?1370614437

[13] http://www.theguardian.com/business/2013/sep/05/walmart-workers-strike-us-thursday

Those of us lucky enough to earn enough money to avoid all this squalor complacently respond to these conditions with condemnation[14] of those afflicted, seeing those suffering from poverty as little more than "surplus population" to quote Charles Dickens rather than as humans living under inhumane conditions.

Let me declare in no uncertain terms: poverty does not make you less human.

Every person is born with the inalienable right to breathe healthy, clean air free of toxins. We are born with the inalienable right to whole, nutritious, healthy, quality food. We are born needing and deserving to live in safe, sturdy, healthy homes devoid of hazards such as second/third hand smoke, toxic noise, vermin, and disease. As Americans, we are born deserving the opportunity to better ourselves through hard work and education. All people who work and apply themselves need to be able to live independently and securely — regardless of physical abilities or challenges.

Whatever you want to think of me personally, I am worthy of all these things. Unemployment does not strip me of my humanity, nor does poverty. Today I live in squalor and misery under the most unhealthy and inhumane of conditions.

But I am human. I am bright. I am educated, I am talented. I deserve better than this. I am better than this. I am not the sum of my present environment. Somehow I will persevere through this — and so will you.

---

[14] http://www.cnbc.com/id/100883308

American Poverty

We can and must do better. It is time we stop looking down our noses at people and come together to make our world better. For every blessing in our lives is a gift given for but a time. Each decision each of us makes changes both our blessings and our challenges. Even the greatest wealth may disappear in the blink of an eye.

Poverty is not someone else's problem, someone else's pain. It is everyone's problem, everyone's pain. It is time to stop treating the poor as if they deserve the conditions they (we) live in, an inconvenience to our pride.

All people are human. It is time we treat each other that way.

Shaming Poverty: One Person's Stereotypes Leads to Personal Humiliation While Buying Food

Myths Concerning Unemployed, Poor Persist Despite Prolonged Great Recession

Saturday 26th October. After working all week at my holiday temp job, I go to my neighbourhood Dollar General to buy some milk and a couple frozen dinners for work. Earlier this month I stocked up on groceries, knowing my work schedule offered little time for cooking, reducing my food stamp total to less than $15 for the rest of the month.

At checkout, my total exceeds my remaining balance by about three dollars — nothing major — until the clerk asked me a question no one asked me since I was six years old buying a soda from my allowance. "Do you have money to pay for that?" she snarled unapologetically.

What? I thought to myself, keenly aware she was talking about just three dollars and change.

Caught off guard, I replied yes simply, showing her my debit card while she scowled over the split payment transaction. Leaving the store, the humiliation set in. Despite my professional dress and demeanour, this woman assumed (incorrectly) that I had no way to pay the three dollar balance owed, something no one ever communicated to me since I was a child buying small items from my allowance. Across dozens of mixed food and non-food purchases at the same store, my capacity to pay for the non-food items never came into question — until this purchase.

So why assume I could not pay — especially in face of my clean, well-cared for clothes and professional conduct?

The answer has to be rooted in persisting stereotypes[15] about the poor, working poor, and unemployed. Despite the length of this Great Recession and high unemployment numbers[16], especially here in western Pennsylvania where the unemployment rate in August was 8.7% (1.4% higher than the national average, and 1% above the Pennsylvania average), our culture still equates poverty with laziness, criminal activity, mental illness, and drug addiction — none of which apply to me, something self-evident in my prolific writing work.

On the flip side, my white cane leads to the assumption by those with little experience with the differently abled that my sight loss is sufficient for me to be dependent on federal disability payments. Few people realize that the federal definition of "legally blind" is 20/200 vision — compared with Pennsylvania's 20/70 threshold for "low vision" which my 20/80 vision meets.

---

[15] http://thetandd.com/news/opinion/legislation-aimed-at-unemployed-feeds-stereotypes/article_a82065de-3efe-11e1-a04e-0019bb2963f4.html

[16]

http://www.deptofnumbers.com/unemployment/pennsylvania/johnstown

That is to say, I'm too blind to drive and too blind to work in industrial settings (where most of the few local jobs are) — but not blind enough to receive cash assistance from the federal government, Instead, the assistance I've received comes through Pennsylvania's vocational rehabilitation program offering me some adaptive technologies (such as my white cane, large ruled paper, and a special desk lamp) designed to help me re-enter the work place.

No matter how you cut it, the words cut sharply at my pride. For I understand that while abuse of unemployment assistance, food stamps, and other programs designed to support the poor happens, the number of people who actually fit the stereotypes are very small — despite what politicians may claim. Most people receiving food stamps do so because the alternative is starving, not because they do not want to buy their own food.

Given a fair chance, most people receiving government assistance would prefer not to — regardless of age. Ask anyone struggling to scrape by on social security if they would rather be living off saved money in a pension or IRA — or off social security and nearly every person would prefer the former. Ask any long term unemployed person if she or he would rather be working or trying to make do through the help of others and nearly every person would rather be working. Ask any person working for minimum wage and not able to feed her or his family despite working full time if she or he wants food stamps and you will also hear a resounding "No!"

American Poverty

Americans do not want entitlements. Americans want to pay their own way. We want jobs and living wages. We want to support ourselves. And we want the system to be fair — rewarding hard work, education, and good choices instead of bad choices. For it is truly ironic that a heroin addict on the street readily gets disability assistance from the federal government — something that person chose to do — but my sight loss and hearing loss only affords me scorn and shame.

We can and must do better.

Public Housing: The Hassles That Should Never Be

Denying the Poor Access to the Basics of Life

There are certain things that most of us take for granted will be routine in our lives: picking up the mail from our mailboxes; transitioning from outside of our homes to inside of our homes; the ability to open the windows to our homes on a sunny day; quiet surroundings at bedtime; healthy air to breathe.

But if you live in one of the thousands of public housing buildings across the United States, none of these can be taken for granted as I found out by moving to public housing in September, 2012.

The purpose of public housing, also called low income or affordable housing is pretty basic: provide clean, safe, and affordable homes (usually apartments) to those unable to afford traditional housing costs. By providing affordable homes to the poor, municipalities combat not only homelessness, but encourage employment, enrolment in schools among poor children, and greatly reduce crime. That is the theory anyway. The reality, however, is very different.

Safety

Low income housing tends to be located in high crime areas. Far from being the safe havens we all aspire to when going home, drug use, murders, and burglaries plague these residential areas. I myself was in constant fear of my safety during the year I lived in a public housing neighbourhood on the west side of Johnstown Pennsylvania – not only from the above, but also from the toxic air I breathed. As I wrote about in my article on third-hand smoke[17] (smoke inhaled from a room other than the one where the smoker is located), all air is shared, especially in adjacent residences. What you do in your own home affects your neighbours – and can make them sick or even kill them. This means that if your neighbour consumes drugs — legal or illegal — your quality of life diminishes. Add in the constant flow of drug dealers and drug buyers on my block and the safety problem becomes evident. Since moving in September to a different public housing building in a different part of town, the local news has reported no less than ten murders within four blocks of the home I left just a few months ago.

<u>Maintenance</u>

Unlike traditional housing where landlords have a profit incentive to keep homes and public areas well maintained and in constant working order, public housing lacks this incentive. This means doing whatever is cheapest – like installing refurbished – not new – elevators into buildings at the cost of resident safety. These elevators are naturally more prone to break downs and glitches than new elevators.

---

[17] http://peersofbeinan.wordpress.com/2014/07/18/third-hand-smoke-the-hidden-danger-to-apartment-living/

With unreliable elevators and a natural discomfort being in closed spaces, it is difficult for anyone in my building to actually leave our homes and the floors we live in/on. Every single ride risks a malfunction which could easily be addressed by simply installing brand new equipment and conducting the same routine care given to for-profit apartment buildings.

Why the difference? Money. Proper care of elevators and other essentials (like furnaces) costs money, money not recouped entirely by rents.

In a time of budget cuts and political posturing against "entitlements," providers of low-income housing simply do not have the money to provide the services everyone else takes for granted. When you realize that buildings like mine are specifically for the elderly, differently abled (including veterans), and the poor, the message is loud and clear about our value to our society. We are not worth, in the minds of others, the decency of working elevators let alone well maintained homes.

Access to mail, essential services

Dovetailing with maintenance issues is access to basic services – like the mail. Because I cannot know any time I get on the elevator that I will safely reach the ground and be able to return without incident, I cannot check my mail every day. Packages are not delivered to each apartment. Instead, residents must wait by the mail box banks for the letter carrier – sometimes for hours at a time – in order to receive a package. Likewise, receiving deliveries of any kind — like a pizza or other delivered food — becomes a real challenge. When you add in the difficulties leaving/returning the apartment, this cuts off residents from access to needed goods/services – like food, medicine, and clothing.

Windows

A very basic component to any home is windows to let in fresh air. However the screens on the windows in my apartment and those of my neighbours have gaps that insects – especially bees and wasps – readily penetrate. On a lower floor, replacing and repairing the screens would be fairly easy – but not fifteen stories up. This means the only way I can keep the bugs out (who wants wasps buzzing around in the living room or in your bedroom?) is by sealing my apartment, keeping all windows tightly locked. Should an insect penetrate that (and yes, some have), I cannot expect assistance from the building. When I tried once the answer was "well just kill the bug yourself."

All of these areas are things most people take for granted. Yet people in affordable, public housing cannot take them for granted. Safety, access to the outside world, mail/package collection, and yes, windows are all basics to life that I feel no person, no matter how poor, should be denied unrestricted access to. Indeed it is a mark of shame on our society that anyone has to think about these things at all. Every single person has the right to live free and safe in homes that are truly safe from all hazards.

Next time you hear a politician talk about "entitlements" think about these things and recognize the human picture. Most people in public housing are decent and wonderful people. Huge numbers of them have served in the military or are elderly. Is this the life you want for your (older) family members, for yourself, for anyone?

It is time to stop blaming the poor for poverty and start investing again in people. We can and must do better than this! Sub-standard housing must become a thing of the past.

Poverty and the Perception of "Blurred" Sexual Lines

In 2013, Robin Thicke's song "Blurred Lines" highlighted American rape culture with its message that when a woman says "no" to something, she does not really mean it. The naked women parading across his video made it perfectly clear where the lines, to him, are most blurred.

It is easy to look at the song — and all the controversy it created — and chalk it up to a mediocre "musician" playing a publicity stunt, a stunt that had Mr. Thicke laughing all the way to the bank.

Except I'm not laughing and nor should any woman anywhere in the world.

The problem is not the video, of course, but what it represents: a culture where women do not need to be respected, where men believe "no" means "not yet," and where that "not yet" is easily changed to "yes" if the man simply pursues aggressively enough.

Among the affluent, this culture has very little meaning. With enough wealth and power, a woman can live her life feeling reasonably safe because she can hire protection for every aspect of her life. While we do hear of celebrity stalkings, they are rarely fatal. Money can buy safety and security.

But what about the rest of us, especially the poor? What about the millions of impoverished women who are struggling just to buy food and pay rent? Especially in low income housing where crime rates are higher, women find themselves vulnerable. Police department budgets are strained; they don't have the money or manpower to truly "serve and protect" as they are mandated. Sexual harassment, rape, and so forth are just not worth responding to in the minds and budgets of the police when there are drug offenses, murders, and so forth to respond to.

In our predatory sexual culture poor women are forced to fend for themselves. Like when a simple act of politeness to a neighbour is taken as an invitation for sex. Say no, I am not interested and the advances do not go away. Why should they? If women do not actually mean "no" when they say it, it becomes in the interest of the man to keep pushing — to force his way into her life, into her mind. That these advances obviously frighten her is not important.

Nowhere in American culture are such obvious communications actually deterrent. American culture says that women *always want it — from anyone who seeks it.* And worst of all: there is no perception that there are any negative consequences. Not to sexual harassment. Not to rape. After all, who cares if a poor woman is violated? Ignore the crime and nothing bad will happen — to criminal or to law enforcement. And when (not if) a predatory man with a mind that says "you have nothing to lose" violates a woman's dignity, it remains easier for all involved or near the woman to simply claim "she had it coming to her."

Because for the poor, there is no such thing as "no," no right to refusal. No human dignity.

We must stop tolerating this. Men must stand up and start caring again about the dignity of women, to stop being predators and become protectors — not in the sense that women are objects to be own (that itself is predatory), but in the sense that human life has value — rich or poor.

Old Fashioned respect needs to return. For every person deserves respect. Every life is sacred.

PART TWO: ADDRESSING POVERTY

So what are the consequences of these conditions explored in part one? Why should we care if a poor woman is raped or sexually harassed? Why should those who are not in poverty care about public housing conditions, let alone stereotypes about the poor? Why does it matter how much a given family receives in nutritional assistance? Why care about the hardships experienced by the unemployed or those working for minimum wage? Isn't there some measure of personal responsibility in all this? Haven't the wealthy and middle-classed gotten to where they are because they earned it through their own efforts? Don't the rich and middle class deserve better than the poor?

Once upon a time when I lived in Lincoln, Nebraska I carried the official Republican Party line about poverty, wealth, and politics. I believed that Reaganomics was good for the United States, rarely questioning the teachings of my family members who to this day are loyal to the Republican Party. I believed that most of those on welfare were on welfare because they made bad decisions. And yes, I looked down as a teenager on those receiving food stamps, believing like those around me that even if you were hungry, it was shameful to ask for help feeding your family.

Then I got out into the world—as university graduates must—and found myself working assorted minimum wage jobs, robbing Peter to pay Paul and living on credit cards because working 40 hours per week at minimum wage did not earn me enough money to pay rent, utilities, transportation to work, and food.

In July 2000 I moved to a suburb of Newark New Jersey that was walking distance to an express commuter train station and close to several bus routes. It was a good town to live in if you do not drive—except for the drugs, gangs, and lack of ethnic diversity which made my naturally auburn hair flame out compared to those around me.

From there, I worked in the much more affluent Livingston New Jersey in what felt like a respectable job as a market research interviewer. Respectable except for the minimum wage pay that drove me into debt, nearly bankrupted me, and had me working seven to ten hours per day thirty days per month for over four years straight with only major holidays off –without pay.

This was not flipping burgers (our stereotype of minimum wage work). It wasn't selling on the floor of a retail store (our stereotype of an entry-level job). It was recruiting shoppers to test products, then running the tests and collecting the opinion data for which respondents were financially compensated.

Mall recruiting and pay rate aside, I found it a nice application of my bachelor's in psychology. The studies were fun and I enjoyed seeing potential products we tested in the office become real products in the stores. If not for that pesky detail of the pay and the constant threat that our office might shut down (and did in 2006, around 18 months after I left), I could have worked there long term. It was fun, fulfilling work. It was a job that decades ago could have become a profession.

Professions are lost in the low pay sector. When you cannot pay all your bills every month because no number of hours worked will actually cover even the basics (forget about Christmas, Yule, or Hanukkah presents in December – for anyone), you have little choice but to work while looking for work – and losing precious pay when called in for an interview with a potentially higher paying alternative. I did these jobs as a single person, with only a couple birds as my dependents. How anyone does this and parents is completely beyond me.

Can it be any wonder then that in 2012 46.5 million Americans including 26.5 million American children under the age of 18 were in poverty with 49 million children and adults living in food insecure households[18]?

In Washington, Congress loves to frame the issue of poverty, hunger, and its connection to pay inequalities and women in simplified, divisive, and black/white terms. The solution must either come entirely from the government (as it was under FDR's New Deal) or from the private section via charities like Feeding America.

But is this fair? In this next section, I will take on each facet of poverty in America in search of solutions.

---

[18] http://www.feedingamerica.org/hunger-in-america/impact-of-hunger/hunger-and-poverty/hunger-and-poverty-fact-sheet.html

Problem One: Empathy

Why does the top 1% of all Americans possess 40% of the total wealth in America[19] compared to just 7% for the bottom 80% of Americans? In part one, we looked at the problem of empathy in America and how in the last thirty years or so our ability to relate to one another has greatly eroded. Without empathy, the ability to relate to one another and see ourselves in the shoes of those we do not know, we find ourselves calloused. A "better him than me" attitude takes over that drives greed and too often creates a defensive, hold onto what I have position by businesses and the wealthy.

Before the 1980s, the wealthy and middle class invested in driving the economy through job creation and through paying workers living wages. Investment in growing your business through a prosperous labour pool made and still makes good business sense by professionalizing workers and making them loyal team players.

The price for mistreating workers can be and usually is quite high. When employees are overworked, under paid, and mistreated, they look for work elsewhere—even in deep recessions. In her 30th of August 2013 article, "How Much Employee Turnover Really Costs You,[20]" Suzanne Lucas specifies six key costs to losing and replacing existing workers,

---

[19] http://www.upworthy.com/9-out-of-10-americans-are-completely-wrong-about-this-mind-blowing-fact-2

[20] http://www.inc.com/suzanne-lucas/why-employee-turnover-is-so-costly.html

- "Lowered productivity,"

- "Overworked remaining staff,"

- "Lost knowledge,"

- "Training Costs,"

- "Interviewing costs," and

- "Recruiters."

Less work gets done anytime a business loses a worker. Potential new hires, as well as customers, easily discover toxic work cultures. Mistreated and underpaid workers are unhappy workers which are in turn passing on their malcontent, even if unconsciously, to customers and clients. This comes through in body language, vocal inflections (stress can be heard), and apathy. If you hate your job, you simply will not do your best for your job. This is perhaps why the lowest paid workers, especially in retail and fast food industries, often offer poor service.

To make things worse, most of the jobs added since the start of the Great Recession in 2008 tend to be in either retail or fast food where work conditions and pay are abysmal.

As Doctor Dale Archer of Forbes magazine puts it in his 4th of September 2013 article *Could America's Wealth Gap Lead to a Revolt*,[21] "For all the employment growth and claims by many that our economy is in recovery, most of those new jobs – six out of ten according to the Labor Department – are on the low end of the pay scale, which is already much lower than other first world countries. Meanwhile, the top executives of the fast food companies[22] at the center of this storm are among the highest paid in the nation."

High management and executive pay rates demonstrate not only a complete lack of empathy towards the workers without whom the business would not exist, but a complete disregard for their humanity.

So what can we do about all this? How can we bring back empathy, fairness, and improve corporate culture?

One hundred years ago, unions were the solution that brought some of the most important and sweeping employment reforms that most of us take for granted today.

---

[21] http://www.forbes.com/sites/dalearcher/2013/09/04/could-americas-wealth-gap-lead-to-a-revolt/

[22] http://www.nytimes.com/2013/08/08/opinion/fast-food-fight.html?nl=todaysheadlines&emc=edit_th_20130808&_r=2&

From minimum wage to overtime pay to child labour protections, we all work safer because of the Fair Labor Standards Act of 1938, the culmination of over a century of organized labour's efforts to improve safety standards and work conditions[23]. Today, the viability of unions and their benefits or detriments to the economy is hotly debated with entrenched points of view on both sides of the question.

But the United States is not the only country where trade unions remain hotly contested. On 31st of July 2013, Alan Travis of "The Guardian" explored Margaret Thatcher's attitudes and behaviour towards UK trade unions in his article, "National archives: Margaret Thatcher wanted to crush power of trade unions. Downing Street archives reveal Thatcher thought Norman Tebbit's[24] stance on union reform too timid." exploring recently released internal papers from her administration. These papers reveal Baroness Thatcher's aggressive tactics designed to break trade unions in the United Kingdom, particularly unions protecting mine workers while destroying the connection between the rival Labour Party with organized labour. These policies, along with the resulting March 1984 coal miner's strike, are perhaps the most enduring legacies of Thatcher's prime ministry, legacies still polarizing across the United Kingdom today.

---

[23] See http://www.aflcio.org/About/Our-History/Labor-History-Timeline to explore the history of labour reform in the United States.

[24] http://www.theguardian.com/uk-news/2013/aug/01/margaret-thatcher-trade-union-reform-national-archives

So perhaps unions are not the answer they once were to the problem of income inequalities and poverty, their relevance muddied by political in-fighting and gridlock in both the United States and Great Britain.

But connectedness, empathy, this sense that everyone has an equal stake in the success of businesses of all sizes does exist, especially in new and emerging small businesses of two to twenty employees. Dev Patnaik[25] in an article posted by American Express agrees, "While it's difficult to build a pervasive sense of empathy into a large corporation, it's easy for a company of a few dozen folks to see the world through their customers' eyes. Small business owners are almost always closer to the people they serve than big-corporation CEOs are."

After citing particular examples from several small business he concludes, "In a troubled economy, where companies of all kinds are looking for new ways to create value, cultivating a sense of empathy is a smart strategy for ensuring long-term viability."

So empathy makes good business sense. But we are still left with the original problem: once businesses reach a certain size, key decision makers and especially those who set employee wages and benefits become disconnected with workers and customers alike, creating misery and destroying professionalism. How do we change this?

---

[25] https://www.americanexpress.com/us/small-business/openforum/articles/empathy-the-small-business-advantage-dev-patnaik-and-peter-mortensen/

Ultimately the answer is cultural. The reason why The Greatest Generation was so good at driving the economy and providing living wages to workers came out of their shared experiences during the Great Depression; they remembered suffering along with the people around them and they felt an important moral imperative to help everyone out. They helped, not out of charity but out of empathy, because they came from a cultural of connectedness. Technology served to make their lives more connected, as it can for each of us today.

The more we talk with one another, the better we relate to each other, and the more we engage in civil debate with those who disagree with us, come from different national, religious, and/or ethnic backgrounds, the more connected we become.

Learning civility, especially with those different from us, is perhaps the first step towards re-establishing empathy and, by extension, coping with this important aspect to poverty in America.

Problem Two: Attitudes Towards the Poor

The second facet of poverty in America explored in the essays is the way the poor is stereotyped and prevailing attitudes towards the poor, including across those in poverty.

We see this in the way I was treated every time I reported any sort of issue to my landlord across two different public housing neighbourhoods in western Pennsylvania. On one hand, the lease requires tenants to report the smallest defect or problem – which is generally a good thing because issues like vermin readily explode out of control unless dealt with at the first sign.

But at the same time, most of the times I've done so, I've been harshly interrogated with "what did you do?" What did I do? A bug comes into my home from outside or latches onto my leg while walking across some grass and I've "done" something? It is an attitude of inferiority, that the poor lack intelligence, that the poor are negligent troublemakers.

Are there some people who really are negligent? Certainly. There are people who only care about taking care of physical things if they feel some personal loss by the destruction of it. But negligence itself is not about wealth. The person with a net worth of $1 million is no more likely to take care of something than a person with a net worth of $1. If anything, it is the person with wealth who is LESS LIKELY to take care of something – simply because whatever it is can readily be replaced if lost, damaged, or destroyed. Wreck something?

THROW IT OUT. But the person who has less takes care of what s/he has because it is difficult if not impossible to replace it.

How many of us who are poor wear shoes well beyond their viability? As of this date of writing, I have ONE pair of shoes, a pair of slip on shoes falling apart which has long lost its tread on the bottom and which hurts my feet to wear because they so badly need to be replaced.

I am not submitting myself to this pain because I like to, but because it's the only shoes I have and I am determined to prolong their usability.

So what do we do about this attitude?

The solution begins with the millions of us living below the poverty line. We must begin changing the stereotypes by genuinely making them obsolete and helping others make them obsolete.

Most behaviour stereotypes tend to have a grain of truth to them in some way which then gets exaggerated and broadly generalized. And of course, this starts with us. Are we taking good care of the things we own? Do we maintain our homes? Are we complacent about problems around us or do we address them? Do we supervised our children and insist they both treat others with respect and take care of the objects in their possession? Do we take responsibility for our words and actions or do we try to pass blame and guilt onto others? Do we live lives of integrity and virtue in harmony with our values? Are we helping others? Are we engaging in random acts of kindness?

American Poverty

These are things each of us can control for ourselves and must control for ourselves. None of these things have anything to do with wealth or the lack of it. They are challenges for every single person, rich or poor. But for the poor, the stakes are higher, not only because we possess so few resources, but because our failures and those of our neighbours have greater consequences to our lives. We cannot afford to squander what we have. When our neighbours behave badly, the blame often is passed to us, even if indirectly in the form of demeaning attitudes.

Community then becomes the solution. We must band together, re-connect, and help one another. We must care about each other and empathize with one another. Individually, we can only affect the perceptions of those near us. As communities working together, we can make a much greater impact until true social change emerges. It is the idea of "love thy neighbour" where you care and you help.

We all know that Congress is not about to help us. But we can come together as communities and address things together. Once we come together, we will find the stereotypes are now obsolete and no longer valid.

We can and must do better.

Problem Three: Shaming Poverty and Complacency Towards the Poor

Integral to our stereotypes and prejudices about the poor and poverty as an economic condition comes the habit of pitying and shaming those we deem beneath us. When we have resources and life is doing very well for us financially, it becomes easy to fall into complacency and lose whatever empathy our own experiences might generate. Once out of poverty, we habitually forget the details of that life unless those experiences strike us very profoundly.

This can be dangerous, especially when it comes to public policy. On 3rd February 2014, the Herald Scotland[26] reported regarding decreases in the poverty rate in both Scotland and England, "The danger is that policy-makers allow these figures to lull them into a false sense that the future is looking better for Scotland's poorest families when quite the opposite is the case." Looking at what he calls an "all-out attack" on benefits to the poor, the report adds, "…as the knife cuts deeper into welfare more children will be driven into poverty."

Complacency makes the problem of poverty worse, especially when we take the next step of actually shaming the poor, dismissing their needs and using our

---

[26] http://www.heraldscotland.com/comment/herald-view/no-time-for-complacency-in-battling-child-poverty.23316022

particular prejudices –like the assumption that those without jobs do not want to work—to justify simply not caring.

But we need to care because there is not one single person in the world who is genuinely immune to poverty and its effects. Not even the richest person is guaranteed to keep his wealth, especially when engaging in risky behaviour.

In the 1920s, millions of Americans attempted to use the stock market to get rich, most of these purchases of inflated stocks made on credit. When the market crashed and the Wall Street bubble burst, people found themselves unable to pay the staggering debts that suddenly became payable in full. The wealthiest Americans suddenly found themselves on a (nearly) level playing field with the poorest, creating the empathy that eventually drove the recovery of the 1940s and boom of the 1950s.

The financial and housing bubble crashes of 2008 destroyed the global economy almost as severely with one critical difference: those who created and inflated the burst bubbles did *not* experience the misery and loss their risky behaviour created, giving them little incentive to change their conduct. This complacency by those most responsible for the suffering of millions has in turn created great anger, especially in the hearts and minds of those who continue to suffer in the form of lost homes, lost employment, lost security, and lost independence.

In 2011 Occupy Wall Street protest marches spread like wildfire across not only the United States, but around the world as the "99 percent" came together to speak up and against the corruption that has isolated those creating the most misery for the poor and middle class from the consequences of their behaviour.

In its 29th September "Declaration of the Occupation of New York City,[27]" Occupy Wall Street laid several charges against the abuses of the 1%, including, "They have taken our houses through an illegal foreclosure process, despite not having the original mortgage. They have taken bailouts from taxpayers with impunity, and continue to give Executives exorbitant bonuses. They have consistently outsourced labor and used that outsourcing as leverage to cut workers' healthcare and pay. They have influenced the courts to achieve the same rights as people, with none of the culpability or responsibility."

Telling the story of the 2011 Occupy Wall Street movement in New York City, Justin Wedes of The Guardian reported[28] on the vicious response by the NYPD towards Occupy Wall Street protestors, "The world watched in horror as three young women were enclosed in police nets and then pepper-sprayed. Across the country, similar scenes of police violence – far from unusual in low-income neighborhoods but suddenly mainstreamed – transformed the national psyche."

---

[27] http://www.nycga.net/resources/documents/declaration/

[28] http://www.theguardian.com/commentisfree/2013/sep/17/occupy-wall-street-99-percent

In "Everyone Has a Right to Occupy Space, Safely,[29]" Occupy Wall Street adds, "It's no secret that the Wall Street 1% who wrecked our economy are disproportionately straight and male, despite countless studies showing the less organizations look like the 99%, the less effective they are. As we quicken the pace of social change, we must be careful not to replicate Wall Street's mistakes. The message is clear: equality means impact."

Equality means impact—across all segments of our societies.

It is our lack of perceived equality (perceived being the key word) that drives our complacency and, by extension, our destructive impulses to shame those we perceive as our inferiors. Shame itself is all about the perception of superiority.

But we can do something about it and must do better. It begins by rebuilding our sense of community, of togetherness. American culture is at its best when natural disasters hit. When towns are destroyed by hurricanes, floods, earthquakes, tornados, and wildfires all differences between people disappear. No matter how far away or close we are to one another, everyone does something to help those whose lives are disrupted, engaging in countless "random acts of kindness." Government usually steps in to help at some point, but only to limited degrees of success. Instead, the most effective aid to those in need are those who are able to most vividly relate to those hurting.

---

[29] http://occupywallst.org/article/everyone-has-right-occupy-space-safely/

This is not to say that government intervention is not necessary. I believe it is. But government assistance tends to be time-deferred; it's rarely immediate and rarely as responsive as communities.

American political rhetoric loves to describe everything in polarizing extremes. But common sense tells us that the extremes are, well, extreme. The middle ground is overwhelmingly the right answer most of the time, bringing together multiple approaches to address the nuances and complexities of our social problems, middle ground lost in our increasingly polarized societies which, in turn, create the very deadlock that both frustrates and infuriates the 99%.

And this of course is how we address complacency, shame, and prejudices towards the poor. Because there is not a single approach or solution to this problem. Every person is different. Every life is different. What will most help one family rise back into the middle class will do nothing to help another.

But what is clear is this: the more we see each other as equals, the more capable we are to address the causes of poverty both generally and individually. This begins by dispelling the myths that create shame and complacency, understanding that poverty has changed over the years. A 19th century model and construct about poverty is outdated.

American Poverty

Instead we must modernize our thinking to accept and cope with the realities of our 21st century world, a world dominated by technology and global connectivity. One hundred years ago, the typical traveller between New York City and London travelled by ship over the span of days or weeks. Today a flight between JFK in New York City and London Heathrow takes a matter of just hours, even accounting for the time differences. Poverty is not about wanting a job or not or how many hours a person is willing or able to work. It is not even about education, assuming the individual reaches a minimum threshold. Poverty has grown more complicated than that.

Let us therefore embrace these complexities, recognize there is no longer a single profile or face to poverty and, by extension, hunger. Our stereotypes about the poor, many of them derived from images of the poor in other countries, must be abandoned. The types of clothes someone wears, the speech one uses, even the level of wear/tear in a person's belongings or clothing do not accurately reflect wealth. One of the richest people I have ever met in terms of net worth washed his shirts and trousers less than four times a year, sat on a couch fifteen years old, and never bought new clothing unless a given article literally fell apart.

By contrast, some of the poorest people I have ever known carefully wash their clothing by hand on a weekly basis, ironing everything to perfection and always looking sharp and professional, no matter where they go or what they are doing, their grooming flawless. You would never know from their conduct that they only ate once in that day because they spent their food money on the electric bill or on medicine. You would never know that the clothing they wore was many years old and perhaps only one of three sets of clothing owned.

And this is why our stereotypes must go. Because you really cannot accurately tell by looking at someone whether she or he is rich or poor. Appearances are deceiving.

Recognizing this, we empower ourselves to care for one another, seeing ourselves as the equals we truly are.

Problem Four: Public Housing

In part one I described in detail several problems I observed over two years living in public housing in western Pennsylvania. These problems include locations in/around areas of rampant crime and/or drug abuse, poorly maintained apartments and common areas to apartment buildings, reduced and/or minimal access to mail delivery services, and reduced/non-existent use of windows.

In our polarized society, we too often take polarized positions when it comes to these problems. On one hand, it is easy to argue that the poor, by virtue of not having vast sums of money to spend on housing, transportation, food, and so forth, should be content with what they can afford. Put up and shut up. You want better? Pay for it yourself. This is a position which correlates wealth with human worth and dignity. *The rich are simply better people than everyone else.*

But are the rich truly better? Do any of us in the 99% really truly believe they are? Or do we side with our heroine Boudicca[30] when she fought to purge Britannia from the oppressive elitism of the invading Romans? Would we still remember Queen Boudicca and love her nearly two thousand years after her death in 61 CE if we did not share her Celtic values of freedom

---

[30] http://www.amazon.com/Boudicca-Britains-Queen-Legendary-History-ebook/dp/B00J43RCN2

and equality for all people? Why do we celebrate Boudicca with an annual fair in Kings Cross in London (UK) if some part of us did not agree with her values and passion for individual liberty?

It is precisely because we do agree with Boudicca that we must therefore address the issues of public housing and, by extension, public infrastructure. As the ones who benefit most from these investments, it only makes sense for us to come together and make life better for everyone.

How does investing in better housing for the poor make everyone better? Besides the increasing disappearance of the middle class pushing more and more of us below the poverty line, investing in the poor ultimately saves us money à la the "an ounce of prevention" common sense cliché.

In 2013, the Institution of Mechanical Engineers[31] recommended what it calls building resilience, "In the long term such action also leads to reduced overall economic impact, in that every $1 spent on building preparedness and resilience can save as much as $4 in relief, recovery and reconstruction later."

Building resilience amounts to building quality housing, buildings, and other infrastructure from the onset rather than taking short term shortcuts that ultimately cost much more down the road, especially when [natural] disasters strike. It's a long term verses short term view. It involves investing today to save

---

[31] http://www.imeche.org/docs/default-source/knowledge/natural-disasters-saving-lives-today-building-resilience-for-tomorrow.pdf?sfvrsn=0

time, money, and lives later, investing in the public good as opposed to what is good for the 1% who want for nothing anyway.

But building resilience is not just about natural disasters (the context of the IME's recommendations). Better buildings and better infrastructure dramatically improve our quality of life. Well-built homes of all configurations are not only safer in severe weather, but simply nicer places to live. They are quieter, warmer in winter, cooler in summer, more energy efficient, and more comfortable.

Comfort matters because of the way it affects us physically and psychologically. It is far easier to be more civil, kinder, more generous, and more helpful to other people when we do not feel stressed, when we feel at ease, especially at home. Our housing affects our health. The poorly built home that lets in noise from our neighbours destroys our ability to sleep without which we cannot be healthy.

Healthcare is of course that other infrastructure elephant in the room. Congress seems to be hell bent on destroying healthcare reforms, the idea being that it costs too much to invest in Obamacare's preventative medicine provisions.

But is preventative care really as expensive as some politicians would have the 99% in America believe?

Two years ago Gina Kolata of the New York Times reported in her article *A Long View on Health Care: Think Like an Investor*[32], "The question [whether or not to invest in preventative healthcare] should not be zero sum. We should invest where we make our highest returns. We should put our money wherever there is a very high positive return, and where there isn't a high positive return, we should think hard about investing."

In other words, there are areas where investment in preventative healthcare services make more sense than others. It is not nearly as black and white as lawmakers and politicians would have us believe.

But what is clear is that doing nothing, keeping the status quo is unacceptable. As discussed in the previous discussion about shaming poverty, *any of us can find ourselves in desperate financial circumstances at any time.* What we possess is not guaranteed to endure—not our health, not our possession, not our lives.

We must therefore take an empathic "this could be me" approach to public housing, building infrastructure, and public services, building our communities and taking action whether our governments choose to act or not.

---

[32] http://www.nytimes.com/2012/05/22/health/views/a-long-view-on-health-care-think-like-an-investor.html?_r=0

Problem Five: Rape Culture

And now to the real elephant in the room for American culture, especially for American women living in poverty: rape and rape culture. As previously discussed in part one, poor women receive less protection from rape and are far less likely to receive assistance from law enforcement following sexual assault or harassment than those with greater financial means. Money talks in general, but rarely more piercingly than when it comes to a woman's body and her rights to decide who, when, and if someone makes sexual contact with her.

American rape culture teaches men that communications from women regarding their bodies are never accurate, that "no" just means "not yet" and that pursuit will ultimately result in "yes" if continued long enough or aggressively enough.

In the summer of 2014 I experienced this rape culture mentality first hand after being nice to a neighbour whose flat is on the other side of my floor from mine in my apartment building. For me, it was all simply positive, civil, and neighbourly interactions such as agreeing to travel together for errands in a neighbourhood where safety in numbers is highly prudent. A form of friendship evolved which again I thought very little of. Being nice to your neighbours is just common sense; it is community and cooperation with others, the kind of things that make life possible.

Common sense to you and me. Not common sense to him. After all, women never mean it when they say "no"—or do they?

In June, he expressed his first sexual inclination. I politely answered with "sorry not interested." He continued, upping the ante each time. Each time, I made my "no" more and more explicit and less polite. He invited me to come over to his apartment and sit down with him on his couch (which is also his bed, frightening enough) to take advantage of his air conditioning. I declined. He continued, all the while affirming that he knew my destiny lay in England and that I will find true love once I move to England.

It was a ploy I did not fully understand until my best friend explained it to me.

Fear set in as pieces in the puzzle fell into place.

Drama erupted after I told my neighbour that I generally do not allow people to touch me physically unless I feel particularly close to him or her; my best friend can hug me; he was not allowed to. This set him off. He sent twelve emails and text messages within the span of about ten minutes about how everything was over. I felt relieved. It was over. I did not call, text, or email him ever again. No means no. I expected this to be the end of the matter.

It wasn't. For weeks after he deluged me with harassing communications. I tried the police's non-emergency number and left a message. They never returned my call or my twitter request asking for help. Since this was not an emergency, I refused to call 911; harassment is not the same in terms of immediacy as someone with a knife to my throat or a gun pointed at me and therefore not worth an emergency call that might make this guy desperate enough to physically assault me.

No, I would not take that chance. At the end of August (after more than six weeks of on and off harassment) he texted me again to tell me to check my regular mail. I waited three days to check my mail after receiving that text, determined to not let his text control any part of my behaviour. In my mailbox was a letter expressing his expectation of marriage and demanding yet again that contact him. The rest I am sure you can guess.

What is truly shocking about this story is that I am not alone. My story is actually rather common place for poor women, especially in the United States. For most poor women, the best and most effective response is to do what I did: ignore it no matter how threatening or in-your-face it gets so as to avoid a more dangerous escalation created by confrontation. Ignoring it does not always work. Many women die trying. But in a culture where law enforcement and legal response to requests for help are too often ignored or excused, a woman's best defence too often becomes avoidance if she can.

It is perhaps the most insidious part of poverty in America. We live in a culture where women's bodies do not belong to women, where women are obligated to give men whatever they want. My neighbour genuinely expects me to marry him. No communication or refusal to communicate from me dissuaded him. All that matters is what *he* wants. My life, my body, my aspirations, and my humanity itself are irrelevant. As author of *Boudicca: Britain's Queen of the Iceni*[33] it resonates eerily; this was exactly the point of view taken by the Romans towards women, especially Celtic women.

Except what he wants doesn't matter. I said no; end of matter. I decide my life for myself —my career, where to live, who to be friends with, and who is allowed to touch me and in what ways. I do not care who agrees with this or not; it is my life to live. I listen to advice; yes, but ultimately make my own choices. It is called being an adult.

So what should we do about this? By now I am certain all of you agree with me up to this point about sexual harassment, rape, and the rights of all adults to decide for ourselves. The problem is still out there and it is pervasive, especially among those least able to protect themselves.

The solution to rape culture begins with the media. Why the media? Because whether we like it or not, the media sets information priorities for us. In 2013, "Blurred Lines" went unnoticed and ignored for weeks after its release—until the media gave Mr. Thicke the attention he needed to run up millions of hits on YouTube—and sales along with it. Once "Blurred Lines" became a story, everyone wanted to see what all the fuss was about—even this author. Suddenly a song and a video that no one cared about became the most talked video and song of the year. Can it be any wonder then that a certain female singer decided to ride this wave with her shocking duet with Mr. Thicke during

---

[33] http://www.amazon.com/Boudicca-Britains-Queen-Legendary-History-ebook/dp/B00J43RCN2

the 2013 MTV video music awards? By being shocking, both Thicke and Ms. Cyrus became household names and best-selling "artists." They are forever famous, no matter what else they may do with their lives.

None of that would have happened if the media had simply ignored Blurred Lines. Odds are really good that most Americans and British would still have no clue what "twerking" means. Until the infamous 2013 VMAs, I was blissfully naïve about the word. I envy those who today still do not have a clue what that is.

Being shocking sells, just like sex sells. When a person can be shocking by breaking rules of sexual propriety—like a video filled with naked women offering their bodies in decidedly provocative and demeaning positions to fully clothed men drinking whiskey—the "artist" is sure to get media attention and through that sales.

But Mr. Thicke did not invent this imagery. Across many genres of music popular today, women "dance" in decidedly provocative ways wearing little of anything at all to "music" which is more chanting than singing and requires little if any creativity or artistry. From Beyoncé to L.L. Cool J to Miley Cyrus, and even Ariana Grande, "music" today has become a collection of mostly naked women moving their bodies in "dances" resembling the gyrations of exotic dancers in strip clubs. Not exactly the dances I remember from school dances in the mid-1980s!

The problem is not just the dancing or even the costumes. It is also in song lyrics (like in Blurred Lines) depicting aggressive sexual behaviour as "cool" and manly and glorifying the treatment of women as sex objects. These lyrics are not just heard once but memorized as "just music," submerging into the subconscious where they shape our emotions and from our emotions, much of our behaviour.

Can it be any wonder that adolescents consider rape culture and sexual aggressiveness normal and acceptable behaviour? In her 2nd September 2014 article for the Huffington Post entitled "The Sexual Violence of Non-consensual Nudity[34]" Jenny Trout explores the social media response to the recently leaked nude pictures of celebrities like Jennifer Lawrence, most of them bashing Jennifer Lawrence for permitting her romantic partner at the time to take photos of her in the first place rather than criticizing those who violated her trust and her privacy.

Noting the double-standard that perpetuates sexual harassment and sexual violations of women, Ms. Trout observes, "Perhaps the most offensive aspect of our conflicting attitudes toward nudity and the importance of consent is that while women are derided for their own exploitation, the actions of a man forcing images of his genitals upon his victims are utterly erased when the tables are turned and his behavior is exposed."

Social media here matters and matters a lot, especially when it comes to the excuses we make for sexual harassment and sexual crimes. Instead of blaming women for sex crimes, our culture needs to support women and take a clear and unequivocal stand against the perpetrators of sexual violence in all its forms.

---

[34] http://www.huffingtonpost.com/jenny-trout/the-sexual-violence-of-non-consensual-nudity_b_5745440.html?utm_hp_ref=sexting

Okay, great, so the media plays a role. But does the solution to rape culture begin and end with social media?

No. It begins and ends with teaching men to respect women; that violating a woman's wishes, implied or explicit, is utterly unacceptable.

When the sexual harassment began, I told not just my best friend but other friends and colleagues in both the United States and United Kingdom. Many of them offered up just "call the police" as if that were really the answer to the sexual harassment. But one friend in particular in England had a decidedly different response: let him contact the harasser and give him a polite but persistent taste of his own medicine. Nothing illegal. Nothing threatening. Just persistent—a deluge of polite messages like "have a nice day." No one can call "have a nice day" threatening, right?

Concerned about escalation at the price of my safety, I declined the kind offer, though I was tempted to accept it. My friend wasn't feeling vindictive in my opinion. But he was taught a decidedly British respect for women; traditional in some respects but also affirming the innate humanity and value of women as equals; civility at its finest. There are simply things one does not do to another person. When you see someone mistreat another person, it is your personal responsibility to step in and make things right for the other person. Your responsibility—not someone else's.

Historically people policed themselves through social mores and standards, traditions of civility and mutual respect that quickly punished those violating those standards. In the United States and, sadly through American influences, increasingly in British society, those traditions have faded away. The old controls have weakened, allowing our culture to disrespect and degrade women with impunity to the point where women no longer believe help is available to them if they find themselves in danger or sexually violated. Rich women have more recourse than poor women who are the most vulnerable members of our societies. But the problem ultimately crosses wealth barriers.

That must change. We can and must to better for all our sakes.

PART THREE: IMPLICATIONS FOR AMERICAN LEADERSHIP

So what does all of this mean politically? In parts one and two I outlined and explored five key areas to poverty in the United States along with some solutions I see each of us as individuals can implement in order to make things better.

The solutions offered in part two focus on individuals in large part because the American government refuses to function, mercilessly shutting down key public services, parks, museums, and so forth that serve the people, practically on a whim. And why not? Whether they actually achieve anything in Congress – or our state capitals for that matter—they still get paid wages that put them at or near the 1% while the people they "serve" struggle to pay rent, buy food, and obtain life-saving healthcare. Not even our veterans suffering from mental illness and life-changing physical challenges following their tours of duty in Iraq, Afghanistan, and elsewhere are immune to the effects of Congress' refusal to get anything done and the resulting 2013 government shut-down, as the 2014 controversy over the Department of Veterans Affairs demonstrates.

Public outcry over the recent shameful treatment of our veterans compelled Congress to actually act—months too late for many veterans—but they are the exception to the rule. Can it be any wonder then that the rest of the world has noticed?

In these final chapters, we will explore how four of the United States' most trusted allies look at and deal with poverty in their own countries. We will contrast this with poverty in America. Finally we will examine how these differences affect America's sphere of influence, reputation, and effectiveness as a world power.

Poverty in Germany

For Americans growing up as I did in the mid-west region of the United States, German heritage and history are points of pride. Germany is home to Martin Luther and a key birth place to the Protestant Reformation. Americans relish in German beer and celebrate German heritage and culture every year with "Oktober Fest" events. The atrocities of the Nazis in the 1930s and 1940s are effectively ignored in this American love-affair with Germany and German heritage. In my native Nebraska, it is German heritage—not British and especially not French or Irish—that people are proud of.

But what is life in Germany like today? How have the Germans weathered the global recession?

The answer to that largely depends on where in Germany you live and what your profession is. Unlike the United States where the federal government sets a floor minimum wage for everyone, Germany has no such unified minimum wage system. Instead your profession and your geography typically dictates your minimum earnings according to Sam Bollier's 19th September 2013 report in Aljazeera entitled "Does Germany Have A Poverty Problem?[35]" Despite this, Bollier reports, "Absolute poverty is almost unknown in Germany; almost nobody has to worry about, say, starving to death even in the country's poorest parts.

---

[35]

http://www.aljazeera.com/indepth/features/2013/09/2013919827574141
1.html

Still, about 12 million Germans live in relative poverty, defined as those earning less than 60 percent of the median income."

On 19th October 2012 Inequality Watch[36] observed, "During the whole period observed, the poverty risk in East Germany was above the West-German rate. While the rate for the whole of Germany was at 15.3 % in 2010, it was below this average in West Germany but amounted to 20.4 % in East Germany." Other poverty factors cited by Inequality Watch include age, single parent verses two parent households, and number of children (if any) in the household. As in the United States, young single parent households with three or more childhood possess the highest rates of poverty in Germany.

English language German newspaper The Local[37] observed the role of education in poverty rates among young Germans, "Typically those worse affected by youth poverty … were teenagers with leaving certificates from Hauptschule schools, the lowest rung on the academically-tiered German school system, or those who drop out early."

Just as regional differences in the United States dramatically alter the quality of education available to American students, German students also experience great variance in educational quality and opportunities, confirming the regional statistics cited by Aljazeera.

If you believe all of this, it becomes easy to conclude that the reason why people in Germany are

---

[36] http://inequalitywatch.eu/spip.php?article113

[37] http://www.thelocal.de/20140530/poverty-youth-germany-study

poor is mostly about things individuals can control like schooling, employment, family composition and size, and profession.

But as with the United States, I urge great caution in drawing such complacent, blame-the-poor conclusions towards the poor in German. Indeed, Germany seems to suffer many of the same biases and prejudices towards the poor and poverty that plague American culture, perhaps proving that though the United States is a daughter of the United Kingdom, her adolescence as a free and allegedly "mature" independent power is far more German than British, despite similarities in language.

As a trained medievalist, this sadly makes sense to me for both Germany and the United States have historically embraced the culture and political tendencies of the Roman Empire far too vigorously and without sufficient scepticism, both relishing ancient Rome without care or much concern for Roman bigotries, elitism, and violent responses to anything or anyone who dares challenge the status quo.

Poverty in Canada

When most Americans think about Canada, *snow and cold* are probably the first things to come to mind—not poverty—followed closely by Canadian prowess in both ice hockey and figure skating.

As enjoyable as our rivalries in sports can be, Canadians and Americans too often compete in the darker matter of poverty and conditions for the poor as well. According to Infographic, Poverty in Canada[38], in 2012 Canada had the fifth highest poverty rate among industrialized countries at 13.3% compared to the United Kingdom's 12.1%. The United States ranked highest in 2012 with a poverty rate of 23.1%, nearly double the poverty rate in the United Kingdom. According to the Toronto Star[39], in 2013, one in seven (14.28%) Canadian children live in poverty with 38.2% of children to single mothers in Ontario living below the poverty line. CBC Canada[40] puts the child poverty level at 13.3%, a lower number based on a different study – but still representing a significant problem that needs to be addressed.

---

[38] http://tvo.org/whypoverty/info/poverty-in-canada

[39]

http://www.thestar.com/news/gta/2013/11/25/child_poverty_rates_in_canada_ontario_remain_high.html

[40] http://www.cbc.ca/strombo/news/10-things-you-might-not-know-about-poverty-in-canada

According to CBC Canada, "poverty costs that province [Ontario] between 5.5 and 6.6 per cent of its Gross Domestic Product. That same report pegs the national health care costs attributable to poverty at $7.6 billion."

Not surprisingly and in common with the United States, housing costs contribute greatly to the misery facet of poverty in Canada to the tune of 3.3 million Canadians paying over 30% of their income in housing costs according to CBC Canada. This in turn ties in closely with hunger--over 900,000 Canadians relying on food banks in 2013.

But there is hope in Canada with The Toronto Star suggesting, "Low-income Ontario families need investments that will lift them out of poverty such as decent employment, improved child benefits, affordable housing options, liveable social assistance rates and high quality, reliable child care services."

On 25th September 2014 Canadian Prime Minister Stephen Harper agreed during his address to the United Nations[41], calling on the General Assembly to focus on improving the lives of the poor around the world rather than allocating huge resources towards just terrorism. Though focused on free-trade, Prime Minister Harper called for broad investments in improving the quality of life for the poor, especially the most vulnerable of the poor: mothers, infants, and children, urging the UN, "not forget to also look beyond

---

[41] http://o.canada.com/news/stephen-harper-pushes-free-trade-as-answer-to-world-poverty-and-conflict

those [matters meriting urgent attention], at the long-term opportunities and efforts that can truly transform our world."

This commitment to fighting poverty in Canada, particularly childhood poverty, has continued under Harper's successor, Justin Trudeau of the Labour Party. In particular, Trudeau's Labour government is responsible for the popular "Canada Child Benefit" which both simplifies Federal child benefits and raises real income for families with children. Simplifying the application process for anti-poverty programs and making Federal programs more accessible to those who most benefit from them has made a difference for poor Canadians, raising an estimated 74,000 Canadians above the poverty line since Justin Trudeau took office in November, 2014.

Poverty in Canada is very much like poverty in the United States—with one key difference. In Canada, combatting poverty is a genuine priority for the Federal government. Canadians recognize the true cost of poverty, not just in terms of overall misery, but in terms of the overall health of the Canadian economy and, by extension, Canada's ability to function politically globally. Instead of moving from emergency to emergency and foreign policy crisis to foreign policy crisis, Canadians see the relationship between the health and well-being of the populace with Canada's ability to function globally, making Canada better positioned to lead globally than the United States.

Poverty in France

France. Whether you are British or American, odds are really good your opinion of the French is, well, less than admiring. Since the Norman conquest of 1066, Franco-British relations have tended to vary from strained to outright hostile. Competition and war between France and England/Britain made stars out of England's King Henry V, France's Jehanne d'Arc, and Britain's Lord Horatio Nelson. So it should be no surprise that poverty in France also has a decidedly British face to it, at least in certain regions of the country.

In June 2014 Hugh Schofield of the BBC explored the often invisible lives of British citizens living in poverty in France in his article "The Many Faces of British Poverty in France.[42]" It is a subject I think few Americans or British ever think about: what happens to British citizens who come to France either as military veterans of WWI or WWII came to stay in France after the war's end, or those who immigrated in France in pursuit of a lower cost of living from that in Britain? As with any immigrant dream, it does not always work out for British citizens in France.

The answer for many UK citizens in France: the British Charitable Fund (BCF) helps them. Established in 1823 and supported by notables over the years such as Charles Dickens and Richard Wallace, the BCF has helped British citizens that most of the world has forgotten about.

---

[42] http://www.bbc.com/news/magazine-27937747

But poverty in France is more than just about the immigrant experience. French citizens are poor too of course at a rate consistent with much of western Europe[43]. With record high unemployment[44] reported in early 2014, it is easy to see why approximately 14% of people living in France, nearly 8.7 million people live in poverty. Catholic aid charity Secours Catholique notes in Laurent Mouloud's article[45] translated by Gene Zbikowski "The impact of the economic crisis and the rise in unemployment are making the people that we help seriously fragile…. They don't have enough resources to meet continuously rising necessary expenditures."

Among the alarming statistics cited in Mr. Mouloud's report: poverty among two parent, two income households has dramatically increased – against our stereotype of the poor. Foreigners in France are also worse off in 2014 than in previous years, reflective of an increasing gap between rich and poor that plagues not only France, but much of the western world as well.

It is a picture very much like what we see in the United States and Germany. But unlike Canada, France lacks the political will to address its poverty issues, preferring the same complacency towards the poor that drives misery in both the United States and Germany.

---

[43] http://www.inequalitywatch.eu/spip.php?article99

[44] http://www.thelocal.fr/20140128/frances-rich-and-poor-where-do-they-live

[45] http://www.humaniteinenglish.com/spip.php?article2369

Poverty in United Kingdom

Finally we look at poverty in perhaps the United States' most loyal and closest ally: the United Kingdom, currently under a coalition government led by Prime Minister David Cameron of the Conservative (Tory) party.

Like the United States and the rest of the world, Great Britain has suffered extensively during the global recession with increasing numbers in poverty and increased suffering from poverty. In Britain, poverty is measured one of two ways. Under the traditional, relative poverty standard (the same standard used by most industrialized nations, including the USA, Germany, Canada, and France), poverty in the United Kingdom has stayed steady between 1998 and 2012 with 2.3 million UK children in poverty and an overall poverty rate of 17% or 27% if measured after housing costs are paid. Not surprisingly, members of Parliament across all three major political parties (Labour, Liberal, and Conservative) prefer to measure poverty using this metric. It looks good and sounds good (if 17% can ever be considered "good") politically.

Shift to the other standard, absolute poverty which is adjusted for inflation, and, not surprisingly, the numbers shift upward. In 2012, 2.6 million children (300,000 more than under the relative poverty standard) were in absolute poverty across the United Kingdom. That's one in five children in absolute poverty compared to one in six children in relative poverty.

What is perhaps most alarming and against stereotype: the 300,000 more children in absolute poverty verses relative poverty are almost exclusively represented by households where one or more parents are working. Despite this, the coalition government headed by Prime Minister Cameron and represented by Work and Pensions Secretary Iain Duncan Smith asserts,[46] "While this government is committed to eradicating child poverty, we want to take a new approach by finding the source of the problem and tackling that. We have successfully protected the poorest from falling behind and seen a reduction of 100,000 children in workless poor families." In other words, unemployment is perceived as the primary source of child poverty by the current administration.

The independent report Living Standards, Poverty, and Inequity in the UK: 2013[47] disagrees, "Analysis suggests that it is low hourly wages rather than low hours of work that are most strongly linked to being in poverty, although unsurprisingly those working few hours for a low wage have the highest rates of poverty."

That is to say, it is low wages, not unemployment, that most reliably predicts absolute and relative poverty, a correlation supported in The Shriver Report[48] with regards to poverty in the United States.

---

[46] http://www.bbc.com/news/education-22887005

[47] http://www.ifs.org.uk/comms/r81.pdf

[48] http://shriverreport.org/special-report/a-womans-nation-pushes-back-from-the-brink/

As with the United States, poverty in the United Kingdom is highest among women, particularly women over thirty, a factor of persistent pay inequities[49] which still plague Great Britain despite the 1970 Equal Pay Act and its modern version, the 2010 Equality Act, "This means women are earning only three-quarters (77%) of what men in full-time comparable jobs earn." Income inequities affect the balance of power between women and men, often with sexual consequences that perpetuate the rape culture discussed in part two, creating a vicious cycle that is or stands to tear apart both the United States and the United Kingdom.

Fortunately there is a proposal aimed at addressing poverty in the United Kingdom from the proposed Financial Transaction Tax, aka "The Robin Hood Tax,[50]" which levies a small tax on banks in order to finance anti-poverty measures in the United Kingdom and across the European Union, "A tiny tax on the financial sector can generate £20 billion annually in the UK alone. That's enough to protect schools and hospitals. Enough to stop massive cuts across the public sector. Enough to build new lives around the world – and to deal with the new climate challenges our world is facing."

---

[49] http://www.theguardian.com/business/2014/aug/19/gender-pay-gap-women-bosses-earn-35-percent-less-than-men

[50] http://robinhoodtax.org.uk/how-it-works

Conclusions

Across this book we have explored the real face of poverty in America from the lens of this author who has lived through it. Are my experiences typical? I cannot say. Certainly they are against stereotype. My life, my situation is not those we typically think of right away when we think about poverty in America. I am bright, educated, and hard working. I am single and have no children. Though I have low vision, I receive no government assistance beyond subsidized housing and food assistance—no cash assistance—creating enormous debt.

For all of this, I remain optimistic and determined to not only survive, but thrive, with big goals and dreams for the future. I believe in myself, in my talent, in my ability to rise above every challenge each day brings. Fear does not stop me, especially because I surround myself with positive people who help me keep sight of the big picture. I am ever looking for new opportunities every day to improve my life and know in my heart that each day is full of new opportunities, new chances to meet new people and discover new possibilities.

I refuse defeat. I refuse to be silent. I believe the past is simply the past –to be learned from but never dwelt upon. The experiences explored in this book are teaching opportunities—for me and for us all.

So what does all this mean? To begin with, it is very clear that the problems plaguing the United States are not unique to the United States, at least in general. Every country has poverty. Every country must deal with poverty. But across our allies, we see greater efforts to provide a higher standard of living floor for those in absolute poverty. In both Canada and Europe, true homelessness is far less common than in the United States. The image shown on the cover of this book of a homeless person sleeping on a park bench is far rarer among our allies than it is here. In Canada, Prime Minister Stephen Harper made combatting poverty a priority for his government.

While it is true that the United Kingdom's official policy is the elimination of poverty by 2020, speeches made across 2014 by Prime Minister David Cameron make it evident that most of this is lip service with no serious anti-poverty agenda. That the coalition government focuses on relative instead of absolute poverty itself speaks volumes, putting poverty into the realm of the theoretical instead of focusing on the real suffering faced every day by the poor whose housing, food, and so forth fall well below the standards we residents in industrialized nations are allegedly living above and beyond.

By contrast, the Republican party in the United States continues to push an anti-historical and anti-history literacy agenda[51] that white washes (in both senses of the word) and masculinizes history so that only

---

[51] http://www.alternet.org/education/why-right-so-freaked-out-about-inconvenient-truths-actual-us-history

the achievements of wealthy white straight men count as history lest in acknowledging and celebrating the lives and accomplishments of everyone else promotes what they consider anti-American ideas—like equal rights for women, homosexuals, for the poor, and people of colour.

Part of this Republican historical revisionism includes the constantly promoted myth that before the women's rights and civil rights movements, before the New Deal, before social security, welfare, and food assistance programs the private sector and only the private sector successfully cared for the needs of the poor. In other words, government-run programs need to go away in favour of private charities and faith-based assistance programs.

Except this was never the case in the western world. As Sean McElwee notes in his 7th October 2014 article "Why the Right Is So Freaked Out about the Inconvenient Truths of Actual U.S. History,[52]" Americans have always used taxpayer money to take care of the poor, a tradition that stretches back even into the Roman Empire and throughout the centuries between. Churches were legally required to provide the social insurance programs so often cited by Conservatives as strictly voluntary. According to Elizabeth Bruenig[53], "You couldn't just not tithe; the Church would get it out of you somehow, and even had specific statutes related

---

[52] http://www.alternet.org/education/why-right-so-freaked-out-about-inconvenient-truths-actual-us-history

[53] Ibid.

to methods of tithing which fit it into the schema of secular taxation." Summarizing Ms. Bruenig, Mr. McElwee observes, "Islamic public assistance was also a hybrid church-state institution. The idea that there has ever been a successful purely voluntary public assistance program is a conservative myth invented to justify dismantling anti-poverty programs in the name of a utopian fantasy."

Part of the utopian fantasy being promoted by Conservatives asserts that history literacy is not only dangerous, it actually encourages students to go join ISIS[54].

Politicizing history and in particular these sorts of GOP agendas that ignore the poor, women, people of colour, etc. is why I teach history through my Legendary Women of World History Series instead of in a traditional classroom. These agendas, more than any other, are the ones that promote the stereotypes discussed in this book, encouraging the shaming of the poor, and undermining efforts to provide proper housing, nutritional assistance, and medical care to those struggling to make ends meet. These agendas are the ones that constantly make it to the floor of Congress and are most at the heart of Republican "reforms" to entitlements that amount to treating the poor as surplus population to be marginalized, ignored, and undermined if at all possible.

---

[54] http://www.huffingtonpost.com/2014/10/01/ben-carson-ap-us-history_n_5910982.html

Even British Prime Minister David Cameron will not go so far as we have seen over few years by House Republications. Then again, Prime Minister David Cameron is leading a coalition government built on both the liberal and conservative parties thanks to European political pluralism that makes it difficult for a single party to dominate government. The political checks and balances in the United Kingdom and across Europe force compromise—without getting into the gridlock characterizing the American system. So no matter how extreme the Conservative party in Britain may pull Mr. Cameron, he genuinely cannot radicalize without disrupting the coalition that keeps him in power.

So what are the global implications of all of this? How does poverty and the politicizing of poverty affect the reputation of the United States globally? That is, ultimately, the real question we've all built up to at this point.

For decades, Americans have used the ideas of democracy and morality as vital planks to American leadership platform globally. The Americans should lead and the United States is the greatest nation on earth because freedom and democracy reign supreme here, with liberty and justice for all! In America, we have religious freedom and gender equality; we do not oppress women and we certainly honour and respect human dignity regardless of age, sex, sexual orientation, race, religion, and so forth.

Well, that's the party line anyway. The problem of course is that none of it is actually true—and the world knows it. Can it be any wonder that many in the Republican Party feel threatened by any history literacy policies and standards that teach the parts of history falling outside of cherished myths about the past? If we admit to the evils of slavery, if we admit to the continuing civil rights struggles of women, people of colour, the poor, religious minorities, and so forth, are not we giving America's current enemies grounds for promoting their decidedly anti-American agendas?

Many politicians would have you think so, that honesty with the world about our own past somehow makes the American people and the American government weak in the eyes of the rest of the world. They would have you think that we are fooling the rest of the world even better than we are fooling our own people.

The problem of course is that *only* the American people are fooled by these myths and these lies. The rest of the world knows the United States committed widespread genocide against the hundreds of native nations that used to dominate North America. The rest of the world knows the abysmal human rights record towards women, people of colour, religious minorities, homosexuals, and the poor that, while certainly improving in some specific areas such as gay marriage, remain a mark of shame on American culture and the American people.

The only people in the dark about any of this are Americans themselves, many of them content to be, as if by closing our eyes and humming hymns we can erase everyone and everything we do not like about ourselves and each other. America has no problems with human rights. America has no problem with the poor. The poor are poor because they are lazy.

This culture of denial, seen so often in Nazi Germany during Adolf Hitler's reign of terror and genocide, becomes the biggest stain on American reputation abroad, especially as it relates to America's treatment of the poor. If we keep deluding ourselves into poverty shaming, into perpetuating the harmful myths explored in this book, if we continue to deny the way gender pay inequities drive poverty, and if we continue to convince ourselves that keeping the minimum wage below $15 per hour we are destroying our economy, then of course the rest of the world cannot take the United States seriously as a global power.

Denial of our problems, especially towards the poor and especially with regards to human rights makes the United States so hypocritical as to lose all credibility globally.

If you deny a problem exists, you cannot fix it—not internally and not in the United Nations where Canada Prime Minister Stephen Harper so eloquently pleaded for global anti-poverty initiatives, especially those focusing on women, mothers, and young children.

The United States has lost its way. It cannot lead because it has no clue where it is going, what it wants (except perhaps power over other countries), and won't turn its attention to domestic policies like poverty, hunger, infrastructure rebuilding, housing, green energy development, jobs, unemployment, or even the minimum wage. All of these policy areas need to come first before the United States can genuinely lead on the world stage again. Until it does, it is simply spending money gleaned from the poor to finance the rich so they can play nation building overseas.

What is just as alarming: for all the political rhetoric given to the role of charities in helping the poor, Forbes reported[55] on the 6th of October that charitable giving by those with incomes over $200,000 is down by 5% compared to 2006 while charitable giving by those with incomes less than $25,000 is up by 17%.

This of course circles back to the theme of empathy that saturates this book. "Lower and middle-income people know people who lost their jobs or are homeless, and they worry that they themselves are a day away from losing their jobs. They're very sensitive to the needs of other people and recognize that these years have been hard," explained Forbes reporter Katia Savchuk[56].

---

[55] http://www.forbes.com/sites/katiasavchuk/2014/10/06/wealthy-americans-are-giving-less-of-their-incomes-to-charity-while-poor-are-donating-more/

[56] http://www.forbes.com/sites/katiasavchuk/2014/10/06/wealthy-americans-are-giving-less-of-their-incomes-to-charity-while-poor-are-donating-more/

It is perhaps this better sense of empathy in Canadian and British cultures that enables both Canada and the United Kingdom to more aggressively pursue anti-poverty measures, to more honestly recognize the huge drag on their national economies that are the real costs of poverty. Unlike the United States and Germany, Canada and Britain have made poverty a priority in order to strengthen their economies with the result being increased global influence both economically and politically.

I therefore call upon both Canada and Great Britain to not only more aggressively address poverty in their own countries but step up to become true global role models, restoring fairness and equality to all people at home and teaching the rest of the world the value of investing in anti-poverty measures.

Until such time as we resolve and truly, honestly deal with these problems, none of the powers that threaten our national securities can or will take us seriously—not in Russia, not in the Middle East, and absolutely not in Asia.

The best counter-terrorism measure any country can take starts at home, at how the poor are treated, understanding that no group, institution, or government is ever stronger than its weakest members and citizens. It is time we stop tearing each other apart, stop playing political blame games, and start caring for one another once more. Then and only then do we truly possess the morality needed to lead. Then and only then will the rest of the world listen to what we say.

We can and must do better.

REFERENCES AND SUGGESTED READING

Poverty and Hunger—USA

The Shriver Report: A Woman's Nation Pushes Back from the Brink
http://shriverreport.org/special-report/a-womans-nation-pushes-back-from-the-brink/

Feeding America: Hunger and Poverty Statistics
http://feedingamerica.org/hunger-in-america/hunger-facts/hunger-and-poverty-statistics.aspx

Do Something: 11 Facts About Hunger in the US
https://www.dosomething.org/tipsandtools/11-facts-about-hunger-us

No Kid Hungry: Hunger Facts
http://www.nokidhungry.org/problem/hunger-facts

NATURAL DISASTERS: Saving Lives Today, BUILDING resilience for Tomorrow
http://www.imeche.org/docs/default-source/knowledge/natural-disasters-saving-lives-today-building-resilience-for-tomorrow.pdf?sfvrsn=0

Poverty and Hunger—US Allies

Herald Scotland: No time for complacency in battling child poverty
http://www.heraldscotland.com/comment/herald-view/no-time-for-complacency-in-battling-child-poverty.23316022

The Many Faces of British Poverty in France
http://www.bbc.com/news/magazine-27937747

Largest study into poverty reveals extent of deprivation in the UK
http://www.bristol.ac.uk/news/2013/9270.html

One in six children lives in poverty, UK statistics show
http://www.bbc.com/news/education-22887005

Poverty and Social Exclusion
http://www.poverty.ac.uk/

Living Standards, Poverty, and Inequity in the UK: 2013
http://www.ifs.org.uk/comms/r81.pdf

Child Poverty Action Group
http://www.cpag.org.uk/

The Joseph Roundtree Foundation
http://www.jrf.org.uk/

Poverty Keeps Growing in France
http://www.humaniteinenglish.com/spip.php?article2369

Poverty in Europe: the Current Situation
http://www.inequalitywatch.eu/spip.php?article99

The Local: France's Growing Poor: Where Do They
Live?
http://www.thelocal.fr/20140128/frances-rich-and-
poor-where-do-they-live

Poverty in Germany Hits New High
http://www.wsws.org/en/articles/2014/01/06/germ-
j06.html

The Local: One Fifth of Young Germans Live in
Poverty
http://www.thelocal.de/20140530/poverty-youth-
germany-study

Aljazeera: Does Germany Have A Poverty Problem?
http://www.aljazeera.com/indepth/features/2013/09/2
0139198275741411.html

The Huffington Post United Kingdom: The German
Paradox: Highest Employment in Europe and Increasing
Poverty
http://www.huffingtonpost.co.uk/dr-mark-
esposito/the-german-paradox-highes_b_4349537.html

Increasing poverty in Germany: differences according to
region, household and age
http://inequalitywatch.eu/spip.php?article113

Poverty Persists in France
http://www.inequalitywatch.eu/spip.php?article143
America Has Less Poverty Than Sweden
http://www.forbes.com/sites/timworstall/2012/09/10/america-has-less-poverty-than-sweden/

The Local: Poverty Drops in Sweden
http://www.thelocal.se/20120316/39720

Ten Things You Might Not Know About Poverty in Canada
http://www.cbc.ca/strombo/news/10-things-you-might-not-know-about-poverty-in-canada

Stephen Harper pushes free trade as answer to world poverty and conflict
http://o.canada.com/news/stephen-harper-pushes-free-trade-as-answer-to-world-poverty-and-conflict

Infographic: Poverty in Canada
http://tvo.org/whypoverty/info/poverty-in-canada

Canada Without Poverty: Just the Facts
http://www.cwp-csp.ca/poverty/just-the-facts/

Child poverty rates in Canada, Ontario remain high
http://www.thestar.com/news/gta/2013/11/25/child_poverty_rates_in_canada_ontario_remain_high.html

Gov.uk: National Minimum Wage Rates
https://www.gov.uk/national-minimum-wage-rates

Wealth and Wealth Inequalities

Wealthy Americans Are Giving Less Of Their Incomes
To Charity, While Poor Are Donating More
http://www.forbes.com/sites/katiasavchuk/2014/10/0
6/wealthy-americans-are-giving-less-of-their-incomes-to-
charity-while-poor-are-donating-more/

Occupy Wall Street: Declaration of the Occupation of
New York City
http://www.nycga.net/resources/documents/declaratio
n/

The Guardian: Occupy Wall Street, two years on: we're
still the 99%
http://www.theguardian.com/commentisfree/2013/sep
/17/occupy-wall-street-99-percent

Occupy Wall Street: Everyone has the Right to Occupy
Space, Safely
http://occupywallst.org/article/everyone-has-right-
occupy-space-safely/

Inc.: How Much Employee Turnover Really Costs You
http://www.inc.com/suzanne-lucas/why-employee-
turnover-is-so-costly.html

The United States is Now the Most Unequal of All
Advanced Economies
http://www.huffingtonpost.com/eric-zuesse/us-is-now-
the-most-unequa_b_4408647.html

Upworthy: 9 Out Of 10 Americans Are Completely Wrong About This Mind-Blowing Fact
http://www.upworthy.com/9-out-of-10-americans-are-completely-wrong-about-this-mind-blowing-fact-2

The New York Times: The Wealth Gap in America Is Growing, Too
http://economix.blogs.nytimes.com/2014/04/02/the-wealth-gap-is-growing-too/?_php=true&_type=blogs&_r=0

Forbes: Could America's Wealth Gap Lead to a Revolt?
http://www.forbes.com/sites/dalearcher/2013/09/04/could-americas-wealth-gap-lead-to-a-revolt/

Empathy: the Small Business Advantage
https://www.americanexpress.com/us/small-business/openforum/articles/empathy-the-small-business-advantage-dev-patnaik-and-peter-mortensen/

Frontline: The State of America's Middle Class in Eight Charts
http://www.pbs.org/wgbh/pages/frontline/business-economy-financial-crisis/two-american-families/the-state-of-americas-middle-class-in-eight-charts/

CNN Money: the Middle Class Falls Further Behind
http://money.cnn.com/2012/08/22/news/economy/middle-class-pew/

Gender pay gap: female bosses earn 35% less than male colleagues
http://www.theguardian.com/business/2014/aug/19/gender-pay-gap-women-bosses-earn-35-percent-less-than-men

UK urged to close gender pay gap and improve participation rates
http://www.theguardian.com/world/2014/mar/02/women-employment-equality-pay-oecd-survey

The Robin Hood Tax
http://robinhoodtax.org.uk/

Unions

Debate: Are Unions Beneficial to the Economy
http://www.debate.org/opinions/are-unions-beneficial-to-the-economy

The Atlantic: Unions and State Economies: Don't Believe the Hype
http://www.theatlantic.com/business/archive/2011/03/unions-and-state-economies-dont-believe-the-hype/72282/

How Labor Unions Work
http://money.howstuffworks.com/labor-union2.htm

Labor History Timeline
http://www.aflcio.org/About/Our-History/Labor-History-Timeline

National archives: Margaret Thatcher wanted to crush power of trade unions. Downing Street archives reveal Thatcher thought Norman Tebbit's stance on union reform too timid
http://www.theguardian.com/uk-news/2013/aug/01/margaret-thatcher-trade-union-reform-national-archives

Margaret Thatcher Fought One Huge Battle That Changed the UK Forever
http://www.businessinsider.com/thacher-versus-the-unions-2013-4

Politics & International Politics

Why the Right Is So Freaked Out about the Inconvenient Truths of Actual U.S. History
http://www.alternet.org/education/why-right-so-freaked-out-about-inconvenient-truths-actual-us-history

Fox News' Ben Carson Thinks New AP U.S. History Course Will Make Students Join ISIS
http://www.huffingtonpost.com/2014/10/01/ben-carson-ap-us-history_n_5910982.html

Parliament: Women in Politics
http://www.parliament.uk/education/about-your-parliament/introduction/women-in-politics/

Scientists Find Happiness Gap Between Liberals &
Conservatives
http://www.huffingtonpost.com/2014/09/11/conserva
tives-happier-liberal-
countries_n_5797938.html?ir=Science&utm_campaign=
091114&utm_medium=email&utm_source=Alert-
science&utm_content=Photo

A Long View on Health Care: Think Like an Investor
http://www.nytimes.com/2012/05/22/health/views/a-
long-view-on-health-care-think-like-an-
investor.html?_r=0

The Sexual Violence of Non-consensual Nudity
http://www.huffingtonpost.com/jenny-trout/the-
sexual-violence-of-non-consensual-
nudity_b_5745440.html?utm_hp_ref=sexting

There is No "Rape Culture" at British Universities
http://www.spiked-online.com/newsite/article/there-is-
no-rape-culture-at-British-
universities/14612#.VBik0fldXh4

Who are Allies of the United States?
http://www.answers.com/Q/Who_are_allies_of_the_U
nited_States

Politico: America's 25 Most Awkward Allies
http://www.politico.com/magazine/story/2014/02/am
ericas-most-awkward-allies-103889.html#.VBshzPldXh4

David Cameron's Education Speech in Full

http://www.politics.co.uk/comment-
analysis/2011/09/09/david-cameron-s-education-
speech-in-full

Crime

By the Numbers: Is the UK Really Five Times More
Violent than the US?
http://blog.skepticallibertarian.com/2013/01/12/fact-
checking-ben-swann-is-the-uk-really-5-times-more-
violent-than-the-us/

40 Years Later: Drug Policy in New York After the
Rockefeller Drug Laws
http://www.huffingtonpost.com/gabriel-sayegh/40-
years-rockefeller-drug-laws_b_3238759.html

FindLaw.com: Pennsylvania Drug Possession Laws
http://statelaws.findlaw.com/pennsylvania-
law/pennsylvania-drug-possession-laws.html

Community Based Policing
http://www.lincoln.ne.gov/city/police/cbp.htm

Bystander Effect: If you Need Help, You'd Better Ask
For It
http://riskology.co/bystander-effect/

www.ingramcontent.com/pod-product-compliance
Lightning Source LLC
Chambersburg PA
CBHW070359290526
45790CB00004B/1565